Mel Bay Presents
Fingerstyle & Slide Guitar in Open Tunings
taught by
John Fahey

CONTENTS

1 2 3 4 5 6 7 8 9 0

Visit us on the Web at www.melbay.com — E-mail us at email@melbay.com

CD Track Listings

Lesson One

Track 1: Introduction to Open G tuning
Track 2: Tuning to Open G tuning (D G D G B D)
Track 3: Discussion of chords in Open G tuning and introduction to *On The Sunny Side Of The Ocean*
Track 4: Performance of *On The Sunny Side Of The Ocean*
Track 5: Teaching of first section of *On The Sunny Side Of The Ocean*
Track 6: Plays slowly first section of *On The Sunny Side Of The Ocean*
Track 7: Teaching of second section of *On The Sunny Side Of The Ocean*
Track 8: Plays slowly second section of *On The Sunny Side Of The Ocean*
Track 9: Teaching of third section of *On The Sunny Side Of The Ocean*
Track 10: Introduction to *Spanish Two Step*
Track 11: Performance of *Spanish Two Step*
Track 12: Teaching of first section of *Spanish Two Step*
Track 13: Plays slowly first section of *Spanish Two Step*
Track 14: Teaching of second section of *Spanish Two Step*

Track 15: Plays slowly second section of *Spanish Two Step*
Track 16: Teaching of third section of *Spanish Two Step*
Track 17: Introduction to *It Came Upon A Midnight Clear*
Track 18: Performance of *It Came Upon A Midnight Clear*
Track 19: Teaching of complete arrangement of *It Came Upon A Midnight Clear*
Track 20: Plays slowly *It Came Upon A Midnight Clear*
Track 21: Tuning for Dropped D tuning (D A D G B E)
Track 22: Performance of *St. Louis Blues*
Track 23: Teaching of first section of *St. Louis Blues*
Track 24: Teaching of second section of *St. Louis Blues*
Track 25: Plays slowly second section of *St. Louis Blues*
Track 26: Plays again slowly second section of *St. Louis Blues*
Track 27: Closing thoughts on playing *St. Louis Blues*

Lesson Two

Track 1: Introduction to *The Union Pacific*
Track 2: Performance of *The Union Pacific*
Track 3: Tuning in Open C tuning (C G C G C E)
Track 4: Discussion of right hand technique for *The Union Pacific*
Track 5: Teaching of first section of *The Union Pacific*
Track 6: Plays slowly first four bars of *The Union Pacific*
Track 7: Plays slowly again first four bars of *The Union Pacific*
Track 8: Teaching from end of fourth bar to end of first section of *The Union Pacific*
Track 9: Plays slowly first section of *The Union Pacific*
Track 10: Teaching of second section of *The Union Pacific*
Track 11: Plays slowly complete arrangement of *The Union Pacific*
Track 12: Performance of *Requiem for John Hurt*
Track 13: Introduction to first section of *Requiem for John Hurt*
Track 14: Plays slowly first section of *Requiem for John Hurt*
Track 15: Teaching of first eight bars of first section of *Requiem for John Hurt*
Track 16: Teaching from ninth bar of first section of *Requiem for John Hurt*
Track 17: Plays slowly first section of *Requiem for John Hurt*

Track 18: Teaching from seventeenth bar of first section of *Requiem for John Hurt*
Track 19: Plays slowly first section of *Requiem for John Hurt*
Track 20: Teaching of second section of *Requiem for John Hurt*
Track 21: Plays slowly picking pattern for second section of *Requiem for John Hurt*
Track 22: Teaching of variations for second section of second section of *Requiem for John Hurt*
Track 23: Plays slowly second section of *Requiem for John Hurt*
Track 24: Teaching of third section of *Requiem for John Hurt*
Track 25: Teaching of fourth section of *Requiem for John Hurt*
Track 26: Plays slowly from second section to end of *Requiem for John Hurt*
Track 27: Discussion of variations in *Requiem for John Hurt*
Track 28: Introduction to *Auld Lang Syne*
Track 29: Performance of *Auld Lang Syne*
Track 30: Teaching of *Auld Lang Syne*
Track 31: Introduction to *Joy To The World*
Track 32: Performance of *Joy To The World*

Lesson Three

Track 1: Introduction to using slide in open tunings
Track 2: Tuning to Open G tuning (D G D G B D)
Track 3: Performance of *Steamboat Gwine 'Round The Bend*
Track 4: Discussion of slide technique of play guitar on lap
Track 5: Teaching of first section of *Steamboat Gwine 'Round The Bend*
Track 6: Plays slowly first section of *Steamboat Gwine 'Round The Bend*
Track 7: Teaching of second section of *Steamboat Gwine 'Round The Bend*
Track 8: Plays slowly second section of *Steamboat Gwine 'Round The Bend*
Track 9: Teaching of third (middle) section of *Steamboat Gwine 'Round The Bend*
Track 10: Plays slowly third (middle) section of *Steamboat Gwine 'Round The Bend*
Track 11: Plays slowly first section and into second section of *Steamboat Gwine 'Round The Bend*
Track 12: Discussion of variations in *Steamboat Gwine 'Round The Bend*
Track 13: Discussion of slide vibrato technique and introduction to *Silent Night, Holy Night*
Track 14: Performance of *Silent Night, Holy Night*
Track 15: Teaching of introduction of *Silent Night, Holy Night*
Track 16: Plays slowly introduction of *Silent Night, Holy Night*
Track 17: Teaching of first four bars of verse of *Silent Night, Holy Night*
Track 18: Plays slowly first four bars of verse of *Silent Night, Holy Night*

Track 19: Teaching from fifth bar to end of *Silent Night, Holy Night*
Track 20: Plays riff at end of verse of *Silent Night, Holy Night*
Track 21: Plays slowly verse of *Silent Night, Holy Night*
Track 22: Teaching of Outro of *Silent Night, Holy Night*
Track 23: Plays slowly Outro of *Silent Night, Holy Night*
Track 24: Introduction to Open D tuning (D A D F# A D) and *Poor Boy A Long Way From Home*
Track 25: Performance of *Poor Boy A Long Way From Home*
Track 26: Tuning to Open D tuning (D A D F# A D)
Track 27: Teaching of verse of *Poor Boy A Long Way From Home*
Track 28: Plays slowly verse of *Poor Boy A Long Way From Home*
Track 29: Teaching variation of verse of *Poor Boy A Long Way From Home*
Track 30: Teaching of Bridge of *Poor Boy A Long Way From Home*
Track 31: Plays slowly opening bars of bridge of *Poor Boy A Long Way From Home*
Track 32: Discussion of origins of arrangement of *Poor Boy A Long Way From Home*
Track 33: Plays slowly complete arrangement of *Poor Boy A Long Way From Home*
Track 34: Discussion of Open D tuning
Track 35: Recent instrumental in Open D tuning
Track 36: Closing thoughts on Open D tuning
Track 37: Performance of *Steel Guitar Rag*

2

JOHN FAHEY

by Mark Humphrey

"I think a lot of us sound like John. He's responsible for bringing these people to life, like myself, who write tunes for the guitar."-Leo Kottke on John Fahey

Time was when the guitar in its steel-strung acoustic incarnation was a kind of chording drum and little else. It accompanied singers, kept time and laid out a basic harmonic backdrop for a vocalized melody. Nothing fancy in it. With few exceptions, musicians rarely turned to the 'flat-top box' as a medium of expression in the way they turned to a piano or saxophone. The classical guitar was deemed a serious instrument by a few aficionados 40 years ago, and the same could be said (with different emphasis) of the archtop electric jazz guitar. The acoustic steel string was for Sunday strummers. In hindsight, we know there were country bluesmen and others who made steel-string acoustic guitars into uniquely expressive and personal instruments, but the role model for most people who took to the 'flat-top box' between the late 1930s and early 1950s was not Mississippi John Hurt but Gene Autry. The stereotypic 'three cowboy chords' would suffice under most circumstances. Simple strumming with a pick was the norm. A 'showoff ' might toss in the so-called 'Lester Flatt G run' which became a bluegrass trademark, but displays of virtuosity were generally discouraged on the steel-string acoustic guitar. It was, after all, a folk instrument, and hadn't Woody Guthrie, the patron saint of folkies, cautioned guitarists against "getting too fancy with your chording"? It was inegalitarian and poor form to show off.

John Fahey was unimpressed by the perimeters imposed on the flat-top box. "These other guys would show me chords," he recalls of his first experiences with the guitar, "but I wanted to compose, because I had All this classical music background." His father played popular songs on Irish harp and piano and his mother played semiclassical and pop songs on piano. Fahey heard orchestral classics on the radio, along with bluegrass, country, and the pop music of the 1950s. He had a good ear ("I didn't read it," he says of classical music, "but I had it in my head"), and with it did something new with the acoustic 'folk' guitar. Fahey wasn't fond of Guthrie's egalitarianism anyway.

"I was pushing to get the steel-string guitar recognized as a legitimate concert instrument," he says, "using American folk traditions, though not exclusively. I was eclectic, starting off with some blues and hillbilly pieces but adding classical licks, Indian stuff, and some other music that is hard to define." It was a quest that could be compared to that of other American musical visionaries-Charles Ives, with his bent and recycled folk songs and hymns, comes to mind. By the time the world noticed what he was up to in the late 1960s, Fahey had attracted disciples (Leo Kottke and George Winston are the most celebrated) and dubbed his guitar style 'American Primitive.' He had also woven a mystique around himself and his music via cryptic/comic liner notes and an alter ego, Blind Joe Death. (Fahey likes to quote Oscar Wilde: "The first obligation of any artist is to strike a pose.") He became a legend, the often grudging paterfamilias of a brood of non-strumming, non-singing, fancy fingerpickers who had little in common with Gene Autry. John Fahey blazed the trail later trod by Kottke and Michael Hedges and dozens more who, without Fahey's example, seem unimaginable. He deepened the voice of the steel-

string guitar. Autry's heirs are still legion (megabuck grin 'n strum Hat Acts are proof aplenty), but the sight of someone sitting down with a flat-top box and picking what Fahey calls "guitar suites" is no longer unheard of. Before John Fahey, it was.

Takoma Park, Maryland is the Washington, D. C. suburb where John Fahey was born on February 28, 1939. In a 1992 Acoustic Guitar feature, Fahey told Dale Miller: "Somebody was always playing the piano (at home), and we sang a lot. Friends came over. A lot of people had these upright pianos back then." Fahey's parents worked for the federal government and, in their leisure time, encouraged their son's musical interests. Music, Fahey recalled in a 1972 Guitar Player interview, "was an outlet for my emotions. I was frustrated. I had been playing clarinet in a school band and was interested in orchestras and symphonic music, but I couldn't maintain my interest playing clarinet. I've always wanted to improvise and write things, more than I wanted to play them." But Fahey didn't formally study composition at the time, nor did he find "an outlet for my emotions" in the clarinet. The outlet appeared in the form of a $17 Sears Silvertone guitar. Fahey had turned 13; his frustrations weren't solely musical. He and his friends hung out in a neighborhood park where, he recalls, "I started playing mainly as a social thing, to pick up girls in the park. I was a really slow learner, and I never did pick up any girls then! As soon as I got the guitar, I started composing. These other guys would show me chords, but I wanted to compose, because I had all this classical background. I didn't read it, but I had it in my head."

Classics, of course, weren't the only sounds in Fahey's head. In hopes of impressing the elusive female, he learned country crooner Eddy Arnold's dreamy 1954 hit, "I Really Don't Want to Know," along with some Hank Williams songs. Takoma Park's nearness to Virginia meant that Fahey was exposed to bluegrass music during the era many consider its 'golden age, 'the 1950s. "We used to dance to it," Fahey says of his teenaged enthusiasm for bluegrass. "There was a special variation of the jitterbug that we used to dance to the bluegrass records on the jukeboxes."

Most of those records were new or at least recent, but a chance encounter with one of the earliest such recordings, Bill Monroe's 1941 recording of Jimmie Rodgers' "Blue Yodel #7," turned Fahey into a record collector and music historian. He heard the worn 78 on the radio show of influential D.C. area disc jockey Don Owens, who got Fahey's attention by announcing: "Now I'm going to play a real old record; they don't play this kind of music anymore." Fahey told Dale Miller: "I really fell out of the chair when it came on. It ruined my life, but I still love that song, that particular version of it." The sound was a synthesis of blues and hillbilly stringband music, and if it ruined Fahey's life by hurling him onto the slippery path towards 'American Primitive' guitar, it also opened exciting windows onto the possibility of mixing genres. Had people always done things like this? Fahey had to hear what else was out there.

Helping him in his search was Richard K. Spottswood, a record collector who John joined in door-to-door 'canvasing' for old 78s. As important as these treasures became to Fahey's musical knowledge and development, Spottswood helped him in other ways, too. "He didn't play guitar," Fahey told Miller, "but somehow he knew there were different tunings, and he even knew the names of them [i.e., 'Spanish' for open G] and how you tuned them ... he taught me more than anyone else did."

Fahey admittedly was no prodigy: the rudiments of fingerpicking came torturously slow to him. He spent some 18 months coordinating the thumb and index finger of his right hand before spending another six months laboring to add his middle finger. While learning "Railroad Bill" from a Pete Seeger instructional record, Fahey was discovering role models amidst the piles of scrapped 78s he and Spottswood unearthed. His hero, he recalls, was Grand Ole Opry guitarist Sam McGee, who made some stunning solo guitar recordings in 1926. "He was the guy I tried to copy the most," says Fahey. "He was so clean and so fast, so good all around. I really tried hard for years to play exactly like him, and I never got very close to it."

Other sounds emerged from the Spottswood-Fahey 78 searches, including vintage country blues and the intense sacred songs of Texas 'guitar evangelist' Blind Willie Johnson. Fahey recalls his first exposure to Johnson in 1957 as a sort of Damascus Road experience that revealed to him the riches of African-American music. "I stumbled on 'Praise God I'm Satisfied,'" remembers Fahey, "which is a really rare Blind Willie Johnson record [recorded in 1929 ... We went back home to listen to it ... The first time I heard it, it made me sick. But I had to hear it again. The second time I heard it, I broke down in tears and cried for about fifteen minutes. I thought it was the most beautiful thing I'd ever heard. I can't explain it, that's what happened." Fahey's passion for vintage American roots music came to include not only the likes of Bill Monroe and Sam McGee but also Delta bluesmen such as Charley Patton and Skip James.

He was, of course, not alone in such discoveries. The 'old-time' stringband tradition was finding young champions in Mike Seeger, Tom Paley, and John Cohen, who became the New Lost City Ramblers and frequently crossed paths with Fahey in the Washington, D.C. area folk scene. In far-off Greenwich Village, Dave Van Ronk and a few others were absorbing ragtime and country blues from old 78s and such then-living embodiments of the tradition as Rev. Gary Davis. The lessons of the American musical past were being variously relearned and the stage was being set for the 'folk boom' of the early 1960s.

Fahey was somehow a part of all this yet also at a considerable distance from it. "I was never that much involved in the folk scene of the 1960s," he claims. His love affair with the sounds etched in prewar 78s was less about recreation (the 'living 78' syndrome) than reinterpretation. Fahey filtered the sounds of the rural South, both black and white, through an internal filter colored by his classical music background. His goal, no less than that of a Charles Ives, was to incorporate vernacular music into a new American art music. "I use a lot of materials and techniques from hillbilly and blues music," says Fahey, "but my overall approach is that I'm playing a concert of suites or symphonies."

Ostentatious? No doubt. In 1959, the year after the Kingston Trio ushered in the 'folk boom' with "Tom Dooley," Fahey started his own label, Takoma, and made his first album. "You could start a record company for nothing, back then," Fahey recalls. The actual cost was $300.00, money Fahey (A) borrowed from an Episcopal minister, (B) earned as a gas station attendant, or (C) got from selling his motorcycle (his accounts have varied over many retellings of this 'genesis' story). Whatever the source of his revenue, Fahey put it to good use. "I didn't know anything about the music industry," he recalls, "so I thought, 'What the hell, why don't I start my own label. I rented a tape recorder, had the RCA custom pressing service press the records, and I jobbed the covers, which were just black and white. One side said 'John Fahey' and the other side said 'Blind Joe Death.'" 100 copies of Fahey's debut appeared to great public disinterest, but unlike other 'vanity' Lps that suffered similar fates, this one became a legend. It introduced Fahey's arrangement of the Episcopal hymn, "In Christ There Is No East or West"

which subsequently became a fingerpicker's standard and was the first solo steel-string 'American Primitive' guitar album. Takoma would become the role model for later artist-entrepreneur labels, notably Will Ackerman's Windham Hill, the epitome of the NewAge phase of acoustic guitar in the 1970s-80s. Takoma's first release was notable, too, as the birthplace of Fahey's con-iic -enigmatic legend, for 'Blind Joe Death' was believed by some to be a real person. In his 1971 book, The Blues Revival, English blues critic Bob Groom wrote: "Ten years ago, John Fahey set out to prove that a young white blues guitarist-himself-could play well enough to be mistaken for a bluesman. Adopting the pseudonym 'Blind Joe Death'he had some recordings of his playing circulated, giving the impression that they were by an unknown Negro. They were sufficiently skilled to fool at least one blues authority, and Fahey had his laugh, but of greater importance, he had developed a blues-based guitar style which, while sometimes rather repetitive, was also personal in conception."

Fahey, however, was not particularly driven to publicize that style. Music was sidelined while he studied philosophy at various prestigious institutions in the late 1950s to early 1960s: the University of Maryland, American University, and finally U.C. Berkeley. Fahey's readings in philosophy (especially the European existential variety) left a quizzical mark on his obtuse-ironic Takoma liner notes and such proclamations as a Guitar Player guest column in which he declared the goal of his music as "Teleological suspension of ontological fixity." Fahey never attained a philosophy doctorate, but such a degree surely helped those attempting to decode his prose.

When not immersed in existential tomes, Fahey noticed the 'folk boom' bubbling with the nightclub perkiness of Peter Paul & Mary at one end and the startling rediscovery of such prewar bluesmen as John Hurt and Son House at the other. There was too much happening for him not to look up from his books. In a 1972 Guitar Player interview, Fahey told Michael Brooks that his performing career began in the summer of 1964: "1 got an offer in Boston to play for $200 a week at Odyssey," said Fahey, adding that he played other folk clubs in the Boston area that summer.

The summer before, Fahey and Ed Denson, a fellow collector, had journeyed to Memphis to meet and record Delta bluesman Booker T. Washington White, better known as Bukka White. "Booker had made a record called 'Aberdeen, Mississippi' in 1940," Fahey recalls, "so I wrote a letter addressed to 'Booker White, Old Blues Singer, Aberdeen, Mississippi.' Booker was living in Memphis at the time, but one of his relatives worked at the Aberdeen post office, so he got in touch with Booker and Booker wrote me." The discovery of White was a catalyst for the reactivation of the Takoma label, dormant since the 1959 "John Fahey/Blind Joe Death" album. Fahey and Denson were then living in Berkeley, and were impressed with what Chris Strachwitz was doing at his Arhoolie label with such Texas bluesmen as Lightnin' Hopkins and Mance Lipscomb. Perhaps a reborn Takoma could do likewise for White, and by then Fahey had recorded the material for his own second album, "Death Chants, Breakdowns, and Military Waltzes." With Denson overseeing the label's business affairs, Takoma was revived.

Spurred on by the 1963 rediscovery of White, Fahey returned to the South the following summer with fellow blues enthusiasts Bill Barth and Henry Vestine (the latter became lead guitarist for Canned Heat). "I got thrown in jail a couple of times in the South," Fahey recalls of those emotionally tense Civil Rights summers. "White cops would often stop us if we were in black neighborhoods and ask us what we were doing." He was looking for Skip James, whose 1931 Paramount label recordings were among the most strikingly original performances of prewar country blues. James was not unaware of his uniqueness, as Fahey would learn. "We found someone in Bentonia, Mississippi who had heard of Skip," Fahey recalls, "and we wound up looking for him in a little town called Dubbs. I asked a kid at a gas station if he knew Skip James, an old blues singer. He scratched his head and said, 'Well, I was in the barber shop and this crazy old man came in drunk, raving about how he was a musical genius.' I said to myself, 'That's got to be Skip James.'" It was, though Fahey found James a difficult character and gladly entrusted him to the care of Dick Waterman, then overseeing the revived careers of John Hurt and Son House. Still, James' haunting music left its imprint on Fahey's compositions. ("If you're going to steal," Fahey reckons, "you've got to steal from obscure sources or you'll get caught.")

By 1964, Fahey was becoming something more than a rather quirky blues revivalist who didn't sing. His "Death Chants, Breakdowns and Military Waltzes" combined, as its title suggests, disparate materials in a manner characteristically Faheyesque. Recalling one of the compositions from that album, "Stomping Tonight On The Pennsylvania/Alabama Border," Fahey points to its sources. "The opening chords are from Vaughn Williams' Sixth Symphony," he says. "It goes from there to a Skip James motif. Following that, it moves to a Gregorian chant, 'Deus Irae.' It's the most scary one in the Episcopal hymn books-it's all about the Day of Judgment. Then it returns to the Vaughn Williams chords, followed by a blues run of undetermined origin, then back to Skip James, and so forth. Most of the pieces I write aren't so derivative." But for all that was derivative in Fahey's music, he was surely the first steel-string guitarist-composer to mix such varied material.

Little wonder that Fahey's next stop was Los Angeles, where he pursued a master's degree in folklore and mythology at UCLA (his masters thesis was on Delta bluesman Charley Patton) and often hung out in the ethnomusicology department's gamelan room, absorbing Balinese and Javanese music. The times were gradually catching up with Fahey's eclecticism: bluegrass music could be heard in popular television and movie soundtracks, bluesmen (including ones he helped rediscover) were bringing hard-edged Delta sounds to college campuses, and a cognescenti (classical and jazz listeners initially) were savoring Indian and other Eastern art musics. The advent of psychedelics and influence of the Beatles would hasten this blend, but by the rnid-1960s we were already living in Marshall McLuhan's Global Village, where Fahey's musical collages seemed perfectly apt. His music was finding an audience, and by 1967 Fahey was recording for Vanguard, the influential independent label which had on its roster both Joan Baez and Doc Watson.

The move to Vanguard did not, however, spell the end of Takoma. Fahey began to record other guitarists with similar sensibilities, first Robbie Basho and Peter Lang, and foremost (commercially at least) Leo Kottke. "It was so funny," Fahey recalls, "we got this cheap cassette with a lot of distortion by Leo Kottke. I listened to it and said, 'Wow, that's great! It's beautiful music, and I bet it would sell.' Everyone else in the office said, 'Oh, no, he's just like you. It will never sell.' But I was running things, so we put it out, and it sold like crazy." Kottke's 1969 'armadillo' cover album, "6 & 12-String Guitar," eventually sold around 500,000 copies (it was Takoma's biggest hit) and gave Fahey clout as an A & R man.

By the early 1970s, Fahey had garnered a respectable cult following. Italian film director Michaelangelo Antonioni was so smitten with Fahey's music that he flew him to Rome to work on the score of the 1970 film, Zabriskie Point. Reprise, a label founded by Frank Sinatra in 1961, had become a haven for hip acts (both the Mothers of Invention and Little Richard were then on Reprise) who weren't million sellers but who had distinct personalities and loyal followings. Fahey joined its artist roster in the early 1970s and recorded two of his most acclaimed albums, "Of Rivers and Religion" and "After the Ball," while with Reprise.

In 1972, Fahey became entranced by the music and personality of Brazilian guitarist Bola Sete. "I'd never heard anything like it since Charley Patton," Fahey wrote of Sete's sound in a 1976 Guitar Player feature, "and this was better." Advised that meditation and yoga were the font of Sete's strengths, Fahey immediately embarked on a tour of what he called "the ashram circuit" which introduced him to sundry swarnis and took him across the country and eventually to India. His pursuit of enlightenment came as Kottke's star was rising and at a time when Fahey himself could have made much of his role as founding father of 'American Primitive' guitar. In keeping with his ambivalence towards fame and success, Fahey chose instead to travel and meditate. Reprise dropped Fahey from the label in 1974, and Fahey was sporadically active in music through the late 1970s.

By the early 1980s, Fahey was again recording for Takoma. 1981's "Live in Tasmania" was his first 'live' album (and perhaps anyone's in Tasmania). That same year Fahey left Los Angeles for northern Oregon, where he still resides. The Takoma label dissolved, but Fahey continued to record albums for Rounder's Varrick label.

Health problems sidelined Fahey in the early 1990s. After some difficult years (he lived for awhile at a mission home for indigents), he made a strong and surprising comeback in the late 1990s. Dismissing his earlier music as "cosmic sentimentalism," Fahey turned dramatically away from his earlier acoustic guitar 'suites' and aggressively embraced noise as a musical element of his recordings. Onstage, he performed brandishing an electric guitar. Not everyone was enamored of this change: reviewing an October 1999 London concert, a bemused Michael Weare wrote: "This is the same guy that pioneered some of the most important advances for the steel string guitar and crafted a shed load of tunes of lasting quality and worth. He has traded all that in for avant garde electrified fence rattling....Fahey can't play electric guitar." For his part, Fahey told interviewer Theresa Stern: "A few of the old fans want me to play stuff that's thirty, forty years old. I just tell 'em to go to hell." But the new Fahey wasn't entirely unlike the vintage model: reviewing his first solo electric guitar album, 1998's 'Georgia Stomps, Atlanta Struts & Other Contemporary Dance Favorites,' 'Entertainment Weekly' observed: "Fahey's doing what he's always done: painting highly personal soundscapes using American roots music as his palette." But that palette was undoubtedly displaying dramatically different shades by the late Nineties. In a 1998 'Wire' magazine feature,

"Blood On the Frets," Edwin Pouncey gave the following summary of Fahey's three albums prior to `Georgia Stomps': "Industrial guitar grind dominates `City of Refuge'; bathysphere-like booms echo through `Womblife.' White Gamelan sounds reverberate through `The Epiphany of Glenn Jones.'"

Though changed, Fahey's musical passions were not entirely upended. He was among the annotators who shared a Grammy for essays accompanying the 1997 CD reissue of `Harry Smith's Anthology of American Folk Music.' At the same time, he was reissuing some of his favorite vintage `American Primitive' music on a new label, Revenant, which he co-owned with Nashville attorney Dean Blackwood. 1997's acclaimed `Dock Boggs: Country Blues' is one of several outstanding Revenant label reissues. And in the year 2000, Fahey's autobiography appeared, a book entitled `How Bluegrass Music Destroyed My Life.'

That title is typical of Fahey's penchant for being whimsical, provocative, and disarmingly honest all at once, qualities which informed his music as well as his pronouncements, written or spoken. Though he said, "I'm not particularly happy that all those horrible records I made are being reissued," retrospective collections of his early work as well as straight album-by-album reissues have kept Fahey's vinyl vintage recordings alive in the CD era. Over the past quarter century, Fahey has been cited as an influence by not only such avowed disciples as Kottke and Ackerman but also by such rockers as Chris Stein, formerly of Blondie. It is difficult to define what, beyond the gambit of putting the steel-string guitar forward as a concert instrument, is the ultimate nature of Fahey's influence, but few dispute his rank among the handful of living guitarists who have changed the way people both play and listen to the instrument. Fahey was once called "the most important guitarist since World War II" in a Guitar Player feature, and certainly he is among the most identifiable personalities to have used the instrument as a medium of personal expression. Though he came to dismiss his early work as "embarassing...pretentious and stupid," each of his 'guitar suites' is idiosyncratic in the best sense: a composition and performance which could only be by John Fahey, someone who grew up wanting to write symphonies but found a Silvertone guitar instead. "I think of the guitar as a whole orchestra," he once said. "It's not an unlimited instrument, but the limits are very high, especially if you get into different tunings. You can do almost anything with it."

On the morning of February 22, 2001, John Fahey's journey ended at Salem Hospital in Salem, Oregon some 48 hours after a sextuple bypass operation. He was 61. His disciple, Leo Kottke, issued the following statement after Fahey's passing: "John created living, generative culture. With his guitar and his spellbound witness, he synthesized all the strains in American music and found a new happiness for all of us. With John, we have a voice only he could have given us. Without him, no one will sound the same."

John Fahey, Monte Porzio, Italy, 1982   *photo by Jo Ayres*

An Interview with John Fahey

with Stefan Grossman, 1982

Stefan: John when did you first pick up the guitar?

John: I was about thirteen and I saw some other guys, older than me, they were meeting girls in the park in the summer by taking guitars out and playing them and singing country western, so I bought a seventeen dollar Sears and Roebuck Silver charm, the action was about that high, and I got to know these guys and they helped me out with a few chords and stuff. But I didn't meet any girls that way until about ten years later. On the other hand I did learn how to play the guitar.

Stefan: What type of music were you listening to?

John: Well, lets see at that time I was listening at first just to country western and then the radio station we listened to to hear country western, in Washington D.C, changed it's format and started playing nothing but Bluegrass. So then I got very interested in Bluegrass. Early Bluegrass is my favorite kind of music, not to many people know that.
But I couldn't learn to play it because you had to play so fast, you know? So I learnt a few country western songs, I bought a chord book, and right away I started writing my own stuff, which nobody else did that, I don't know why. I had a big background in listening to classical music and I started trying to compose, like I was playing the guitar but I heard an orchestra in my head. So I was really composing for full orchestra and of course I didn't know enough chords or harmonies yet but I came up with some interesting stuff.

Stefan: What were some of the tunes in that period?

John: Oh you know the first song I wrote completely was that one I did on today's lesson called "On the sunny side of the ocean". I think I was fourteen when I did that one. See my father knew a lot about music, he played the piano and he would do theory and stuff like that, but I didn't learn anything from him, but I played that for him and he liked it a lot. Then the next song I wrote he didn't like. But that was one of my earliest songs, as complex as it is.

8

Stefan: When did you leave the Washington D.C. area?

John: Oh, 1962. The music scene was so bad that several of us decided to come out to Berkeley and take over the folk music scene here. And there were about forty of us actually who came out. This was something we planned at Parties; ED Denson was in on it, a lot of other people, and we came out gradually, but we made quite an impact here, which was impossible in Washington D.C.

Stefan: The name Blind Joe Death, where did that originate from?

John: (Laughs) Well when I made my first record I thought it would be a good joke to have me on one side, have the label say John Fahey on one side, and this guy Blind Joe Death on the other side. The reason it said "blind" is because a lot of the people I learned from were on old 78 RPM records and a lot of them were blind, and their names were Blind Willie Johnson, Blind Boy Fuller, Blind Joe Taggart, on and on, a whole bunch of them were blind. So me and a guy named Greg Eldridge we were sitting around drinking a beer one night and I was trying to find a catchy name for the other guy and he was helping me and he finally said "Blind Joe Death", and I said "um, That's it". Also I was think-ing, when ever you print the word "Death" people look at it and I was thinking of record sales already even though I was only going to have a hundred copies pressed.

Stefan: Whose idea was it to do a record?

John: Oh, my idea. I thought I'd be wasting my time to go to commercial record companies and make demos for them, because don't forget, I was doing what I was doing and nobody understood what I was doing. Even Sam Charters, I still have a letter from 1959, where I sent Charters a copy of my first record and he wrote me back to tell me how terrible I was and how Jack Elliot and so on and so forth were much better than me. He completely misunderstood what I was trying to do. But that was OK. I understood what I was trying to do.

Stefan: What were you trying to do?

John: Well I was on the one hand, the more I played the guitar the more I began to really love the guitar and to love virtually any kind of music that anybody played well on guitar. In the music I was composing I was trying to express my emotions, my so called negative emotions, which were depression, anger and so forth. Like Stan Kenton did. He got away with it. I 've always admired him for that. I listen to Stan Kenton a lot then and I still do. And I was trying to put together some distant music, I was thinking mainly of Bartok as a model, but played in this finger picking pattern, which I still use. So I was trying to put those things together into a coherent musical language which people would understand and it worked pretty good. Everybody else was just trying to copy folk musicians, I wasn't trying to do that. I was using them as teachers for technique but I was never trying to be a folk. How can I be a folk? I'm from the suburbs you know?

Stefan: Show me how other guitar players have influenced you, give me some examples.

John: Um. Well, lets see. I used to go record collecting with Dick Spotswood and I was just looking for bluegrass records but I found some Blind Blake records, and who else...Oh Sylvester Weaver, kind of an obscure character but they reissued some of his stuff on CD's now , and Lonnie Johnson even respected Weaver a lot. So one of the first guys I heard was Sylvester Weaver on these old 78's recorded probably around 1923-28.

Stefan: Which guitar players influenced you? The old blues players or white guitar players? Give me some examples, show me.

John: Well, in my early record collecting days I was only looking for bluegrass but I found a lot of records like Blind Blake, but the guy who really influenced me made a lot of OK records, his name was Sylvester Weaver, and he wrote "Steel Guitar Rag" and Lonnie Johnson gave him a lot of credit for both being a good composer and a good guitarist, great guitarist, in fact as far as I know of all those old guys Lonnie was the only one to respect Sylvester Weaver at all. But anyway here's one of Weaver's pieces that I learnt off of one of his records, I don't remember the name of it, this may be called "Buck Town Stomp" but I'm not sure. Very simple, kind of ragtime style, he played very slowly. So I learned that song and a few others by Sylvester Weaver and I learned some by Blind Blake and what was interesting was that shortly after I learned a lot of these ragtime pieces I met Elizabeth Cotten, she lived in D.C at the time, and she had a version of the same song that Sylvester Weaver had recorded, and I didn't realize then that she had learned a lot off of old records like I was, but she played it a lot faster and she left the first part out. So I used to take Elizabeth Cotten to parties and we would trade songs with each other and other people. I didn't really learn too much from her in terms of technique or songs but on the other hand we had a lot of fun in any case. See by the time I met her I had already become a pretty good guitar player of ragtime style and blues. And of course she played backwards. Oh, the one thing she taught me was, I was trying to learn to play blues with steel in open G, in Spanish tuning. I mean this had been going on for years, it was driving me crazy, I had learned how to do it in D, everybody I met who could play guitar I 'd ask people how to do that in this tuning, and she knew how, she couldn't do it anymore but she showed me how, and that was to put the steel all the way across the strings. I'm not in that tuning anymore, but to use the steel all the way, instead of like what you do in open D where you do a lot of melodic work on just one string. And that will be in the forth coming lessons. But that was a very important thing to learn and she did teach me that.

Stefan: The music of Charlie Patton?

John: Well, I didn't get into these heavy blues figures until several years later, probably, 58-59. I was in North Carolina, fishing with my father and I went canvassing for old records in the black section and I found Charlie Patton's record of high water everywhere, part 1 and part 2, and it was so scratched that it sounded to me like the guy was playing in a inner tube or something and I didn't know what to make of it so I called up a collector friend and he had that record in mint condition and several others by Charlie Patton and pretty soon those guys from the Mississippi Delta really caught into me. I never really learned to play like Charlie Patton he used to flat pick and his fingers and stuff like that. I never got his right hand but I learned quite a bit from him of chords and harmony things, especially dissonances, he uses that a lot.

Stefan: When did you become a record Mogul?

John: A mogul? Goodness it took years and years. And it just fell in my lap when I met Norman Pierce, who lived over in San Francisco. And that was after I moved to Berkeley in 1963, and I made a second record out here and I gave him as a present my record, I didn't know he was a national distributor, and he said " hey I think I can sell these" and he wanted ten next week, and fifty the week after that, and I was a student at CAL and I didn't have time for all that stuff so I asked him to take over the record company, I just wanted to make records. That's how Tacoma records got started.

Stefan: Your music has been called "American Primitive Guitar". Does that mean anything to you?

John: Well, I used that term and all that I meant is what you would call primitive painters, which just means untutored. I didn't really mean much of anything, I was just trying to come up with a label. Other people took it to mean other things like noise or dissonance or things like that. Which I do but I didn't actually mean it that way when I used that expression. But everybody started using it.

Stefan: Do you feel that you're the father of a guitar movement, meaning Leo Kotke, the Windham Hill school, do you feel as if you were the seed for that?

John: Yes to a very large extent but I don't think ... well what I did was that I was the first one to just go out and just play steel guitar concerts and when I did it I didn't just do it in the United States, I did it in England, and everybody kept on saying " What are you going to sing?" and I would say "I don't sing I just play the guitar and so I was the person who made that possible so in that sense I made the steel string guitar concert respectable. As for being the father of these other guitar players in any other sense, especially new age music, I do not want that appellation.

Stefan: John, tell me about your role in blues research. Bukka white, Skip James, tell me about what happened.

John: Oh well in the case of Skip James I'd heard his 1931 recorded 78's and he played in, I couldn't figure out in what tuning he was in or how he did what he did, I just couldn't get it. So by that time, say 58/59 I led a lot of excursions into the deep south looking for old records, particularly by blues figures and also looking for Pete Lloyd, Skip James and Bukka White and so on. And eventually I did find Skip James and we did not get along very well, clashing personalities, but he did show me what tuning he was in, which was open D minor and he showed me basic chords and he showed me some stuff he's never recorded that I play in concert a lot. Also I found Bukka White who was a really nice guy, we got along real well, had a lot of fun and adventures together. Both these people died a long time ago. And I wrote a theoretical book on the modes Charlie Patton sang in, the tunings he used on the guitar, and the rhythmic structure. That was my master's thesis at UCLA and I wanted to find out what it was about Patton that was so exciting. Because to me he was the most exciting guitar player and blues singer ever heard. So in order to find out what he was doing I had to really analyze what he did. He's left behind about 40 records. He died in 1934 but we have most of his records. What I found was that he, in an approximately 12 bar blues song he almost never played 12 bars exactly, I averaged them all and it came out to 13 and a half. So he was always doing unexpected things which didn't draw you when he did them but nevertheless were executed so well, with such dexterity, that you noticed it, you felt it, he was hot like very few other people and that's what I found the great thing about Charlie Patton was.

Stefan: Where is your music going?

John: My music? Oh I'm getting more and more into Jazz and alternative stuff. I've started doing Tuva singing or throat singing, and ......A lot of the stuff I've been doing for the past two years including Tuva singing, and tuning all the strings of the guitar to the same note, and playing steel, I didn't know what I was doing so I recorded a lot of it and took it around to various record stores and two or three people told me that what I was doing has already existed and it's called Gothic Industrial ambiance and it's a lot of fun because you get to scream and make noises. But I'm not giving up guitar playing per se.

Stefan: How does it feel to get up on stage and play a tune that you wrote in 1959 /1960 and people still want to hear that?

John: Well I do feel a little dragged by that because I'd prefer to do what I'm doing at the time but I also realize that you have to keep a lot of those songs in your repertoire and up to practice. Any professional musician realizes that keeps them around. And keeps trying to get the audience to go forward with them, but they don't always want to go, but that's OK.

Stefan: Lastly, what happened at the time of the Vietnamese war as far as fingerpicks, thumbpicks? Talk about that, about how that affected your music.

John: Well I initially started using Dobro thumb picks, Japanese finger picks, here in Berkeley, I saw Perry Lederman do it, and I like to be heard, you know I'd go to parties and if I just used my hand and my fingernails nobody could hear me, so I started using those and they are louder and most of my records were cut with finger picks. But sometime back, the company that made large size Dobro thumb picks, changed the dyes and this new batch came out and I can't use them. This also happened to you, we both had to change our styles of playing, and went back to just using what nature gave us. I personally am glad because I like the tone better. But I can't play quite as fast or quite as noisy as I used to be able to.

A John Fahey Discography

John Fahey recorded many albums in his lifetime. Below is a partial listing. Detailed information about track listings, original release dates, reviews and availability can be found at www.johnfahey.com.

Album Title	Label
Volume 1: Blind Joe Death	Takoma
Volume 2:Death Chants, Breakdowns &Military Waltzes	Takoma
Volume Dance of Death &Other Plantation Favorites	Takoma
The Great San Bernardino Birthday Party	Takoma
Days Have Gone By - Volume 6	Takoma
The Transfiguration of Blind Joe Death	Takoma
The Voice of the Turtle	Takoma
The New Possibility	Takoma
America	Takoma
Fare Forward Voyagers (Soldier's Choice)	Takoma
Old Fashioned Love	Takoma
Christmas With John Fahey, Volume II	Takoma
The Best of John Fahey 1959-1977	Takoma
Visits Washington, D.C.	Takoma
Yes! Jesus Loves Me	Takoma
John Fahey Live In Tasmania	Takoma
Railroads 1	Takoma/Allegiance
Yes! Jesus Loves Me	Vanguard
John Fahey Guitar "Requia"	Vanguard
Yellow Princess	Vanguard
The Essential John Fahey	Reprise
Of Rivers And Religion	Reprise
After the Ball	Varrick
Christmas Guitar, Volume One	Varrick
Popular Songs of Christmas and New Year's	Varrick
Let Go	Varrick
Rain Forests, Oceans And Other Themes	Varrick
I Remember Blind Joe Death	Varrick
Old Girlfriends and Other Horrible Memories	Shanachie
God, Time and Casualty	Shanachie
Old Fashioned Love	Burnside
The John Fahey Christmas Album	Rhino
Return of the Repressed: The John Fahey Anthology	

EXPLANATION OF THE TAB SYSTEM

"...Learning from listening is unquestionably the best way, the only way that suits this kind of music. You are setting the notes down for a record of what happened, a record that can be studied, preserved and so on, a necessary and useful companion to the recordings of the actual sounds. I keep thinking of this as I transcribe; if you could do it, it would be good to have a legend across each page reading : 'Listen to the record if you want to learn the song.'"

Hally Wood (taken from the Publisher's Foreword to the *New Lost City Ramblers Songbook*.)

These words are most suitable for introducing the tablature system, for tablature is just a guide and should be used in conjunction with the recordings. Tablature is not like music notation, however the combination of tab and music in an arrangement forms a complete language. Used together with the original recordings they give a total picture of the music.

The tab system does not attempt to show rhythms or accents. These can be found on the music or heard in the recordings. Music notation tackles these articulations to a degree, but the overall sensations, the feel and the soul of music cannot be wholly captured on the written page. In the words of the great Sufi Hazrat Inayat Khan: "...The traditional ancient songs of India composed by great Masters have been handed down from father to son. The way music is taught is different from the Western way. It is not always written, but is taught by imitation. The teacher sings and the pupil imitates and the intricacies and subtleties are learned by imitation."

This is the theme I've tried to interpolate into the tablature. Tablature is the roadmap and you are the driver. Now to the tab:

Each space indicates a string. The top space represents the first string, second space the second string, etc. A zero means an open string, a number in the space indicates the fretted position, for instance a 1 in a space indicates the first fret of that string.

In the diagram below the zero is on the second string and indicates the open second string is played. The 1 is placed on the third string and signifies the first fret of the third string. Likewise, the 4 is in the fourth space and indicates the fourth fret of the fourth string.

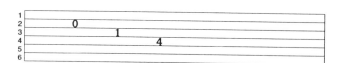

Generally for fingerpicking styles you will be playing the thumb, index and middle fingers of your picking hand. To indicate the picking finger in tab the stems go up and line up down from the numbers.

A. A stem down means that your thumb strikes the note.
B. If a stem is up, your index or middle finger strikes the note. The choice of finger is left up to you, as your fingers will dictate what is most comfortable, especially when playing a song up to tempo!

C. The diagram below shows an open sixth string played with the thumb followed by the second fret of the third string played with the index or middle finger:

In most cases the thumb will play an alternating bass pattern, usually on the bass strings. The index and middle fingers play melodic notes on the first, second and third strings. Please remember, this is not a rule; there are many exceptions.

In fingerpicking there are two "picking" styles: Regular picking and "pinching" two notes together. A pinch is shown in the tab by a line connecting two notes. A variation of this can also be two treble notes pinched with a bass note. Follow the examples below from left to right:

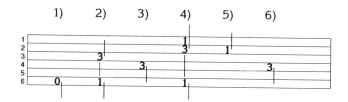

1) The open sixth string is played with the thumb.
2) The first fret of the sixth string is pinched together with the third fret on the third string. The sixth string is played with the thumb, the third string with the index finger.
3) The thumb strikes the third fret of the fourth string.
4) The first fret/sixth string is played with the thumb; it's pinched with two notes in the treble. The index and middle fingers strike the first fret/first string and the third fret/second string.
5) The next note is the index finger hitting the first fret/second string.
6) Lastly, the bass note is played with the thumb on the third fret/fourth string.

There are certain places in blues and contemporary guitar that call for the use of either strumming techniques or accented bass notes. The tab illustrates these as follows:

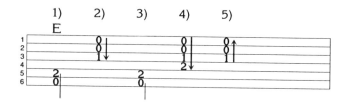

1) The thumb hits the open sixth string and the second fret on the fifth string should also sound. For example, play an E chord. Now strike the open string and vary the force of your attack. Try hitting it hard enough so that the fifth string vibrates as well. This technique is very important for developing a full sound and the right alternating bass sound.

2) Next the arrow notation indicates a brush and the arrowhead indicates the direction of the brush.

   A. If the arrowhead is pointed down, the hand brushes up towards the sixth string.
   B. If pointed up, the hand brushes down towards the first string.
   C. The number of strings to be played by the brush is shown by the length of the arrows. For example, this arrow shows a brush up toward the sixth string, but indicates to strike only the first, second and third strings.
   D. The brush can be done with your whole hand, index finger or middle and ring finger. Let comfort plus a full and "right" sound guide your choice.

3) The third set of notes again shows the sixth string/open bass note played with the thumb and being struck hard enough to make the fifth string/second fretted position sound.

4) Once more an arrow pointed downward indicates a brush up. This example forms an E chord and the brush up includes the first, second, third and fourth strings.

5) The last set of notes has an arrow pointed upward, indicating a brush downward striking the first, second, and third strings.

Here are several special effects that are also symbolized in tablature:

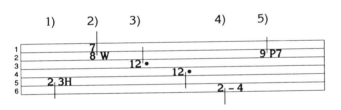

1) HAMMER-ON: Designated by an "H" which is placed after the stem on the fret to be hammered. In the example above, fret the second fret/fifth string and pick it with your thumb. Then "hammer-on" (hit hard) the third fret/fifth string, i.e. fret the third fret/fifth string. This is an all-in-one, continuous motion which will produce two notes rapidly with one picking finger strike.

2) WHAM: Designated by a "W." In the example the eighth fret/second string is "whammed" and played with the seventh fret/first string. Both notes are played together with your index and middle fingers respectively. The whammed note is "stretched." We do this by literally bending the note up. We can "wham" the note up a half tone, full tone, etc.

3) HARMONICS: Symbolized by a dot (•). To play a harmonic: gently lay your finger directly above the indicated fret (don't press down!) The two notes in the example are both harmonics. The first on the twelfth fret/third string is played with the index/middle finger, while the second note—twelfth fret/fourth string—is played with the thumb.

4) SLIDE: Shown with a dash (–). Play the second fret/sixth string and then slide up to the fourth fret of the sixth string. This is a continuous movement: the string is struck once with your thumb.

5) PULL-OFF: "P" designates a "pull-off." Fret both the seventh and ninth frets on the second string. Play the ninth fret with your index/middle finger and then quickly remove it in the same stroke, leaving the seventh fret/second string. Pull-offs are generally in a downward direction.

6) In certain cases other specific symbols are added to the tab, for instance:
   A. For ARTIFICIAL HARMONICS an "X" is placed after the fretted position.
   B. For SNAPPING a note an indication may be given with a symbol or the written word.

Many times these special techniques are combined, for instance putting a pull-off and a hammer-on together. Coordination of your fretting and picking hands will be complex initially, but the end results are exciting and fun to play.

PICKING HAND POSITION FOR FINGERPICKING STYLES: The Classical and Flamenco schools have strict right-hand rules, however for this style of acoustic fingerpicking there are NO RULES, only suggestions. Your right hand position should be dictated by comfort, however in observation of many well-known fingerpickers I found one hand position similarity—they all tend to rest their little finger and/or ring finger on the face of the guitar. This seems to help their balance for accenting notes and control of the guitar. Experiment with this position: it may feel uncomfortable at first. I ask my students to perfect this position and then compare the sound to when their finger(s) were not placed on the face of the guitar. They usually find the sound is greatly improved when some contact is kept with the guitar face.

MUSIC NOTATION: We have somewhat adapted the music notation in that this also shows whether the note is picked with your thumb or index/middle fingers. The stems of the music notes correspond to the direction of the tab stems. I hope this will make the music notation clearer to fingerpicking guitarists.

I hope you will feel at home and comfortable with the tablature and musical notations. Remember, these are only road maps indicating where and how you should place your fingers. The playing and musical interpretation is up to you.

ON THE SUNNY SIDE OF THE OCEAN

Open G Tuning: DGDGBD

CHORDS USED IN "OPEN G" TUNING

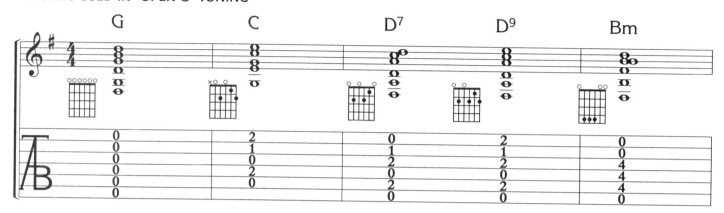

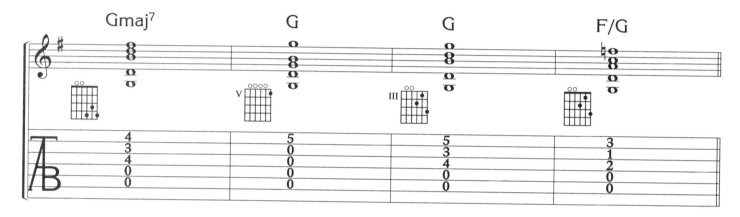

SECTION ONE

Music by John Fahey © 1974 Tortoise Music   All Rights Reserved. Used With Permission

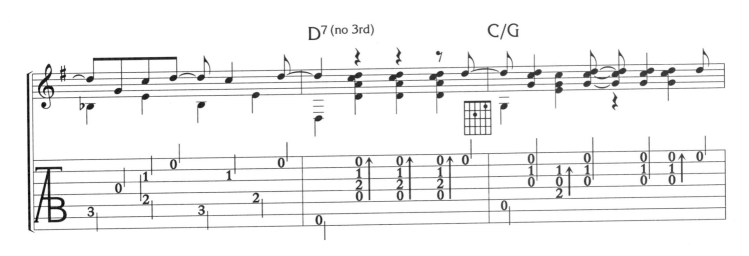

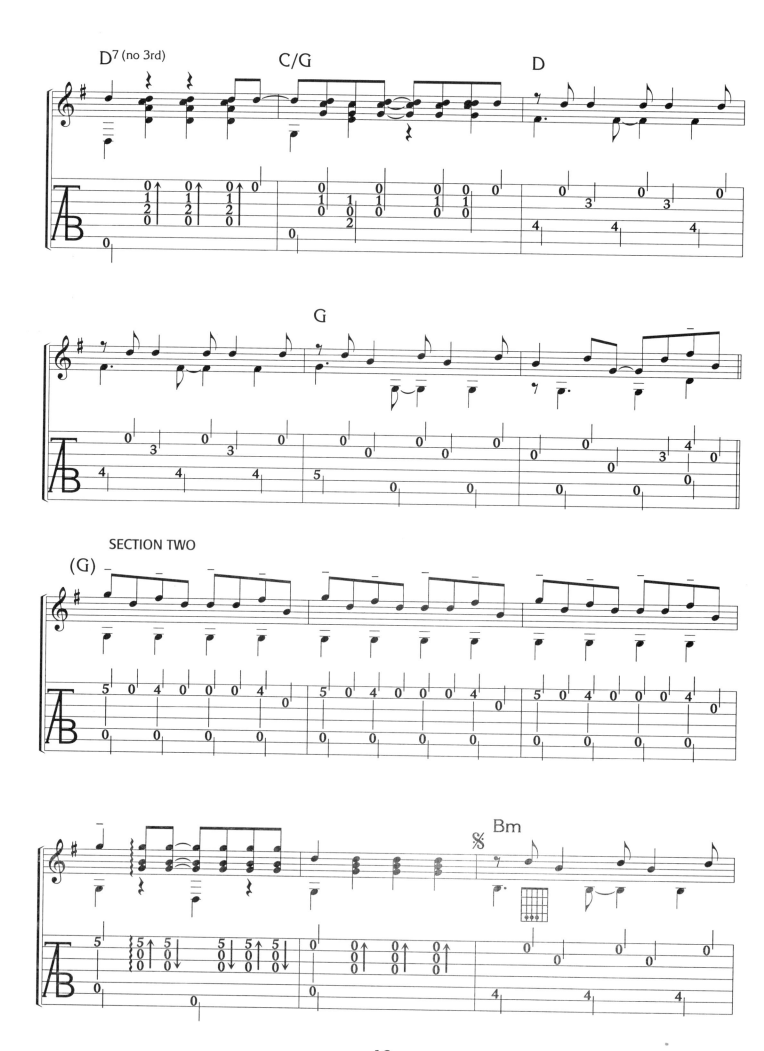

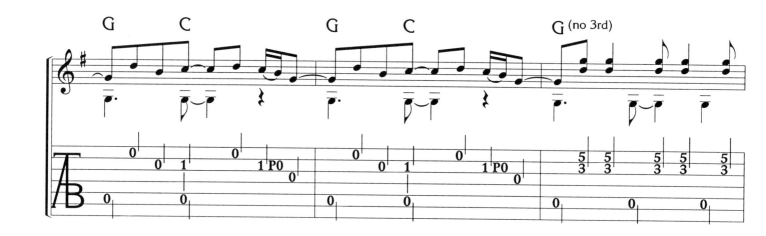

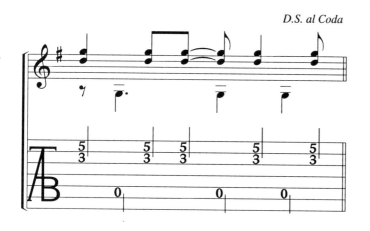

20

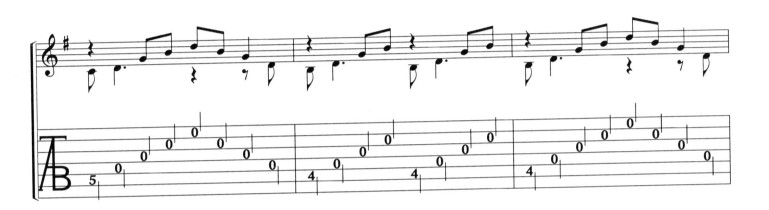

SPANISH TWO STEP

Open G Tuning: DGDGBD

SECTION ONE

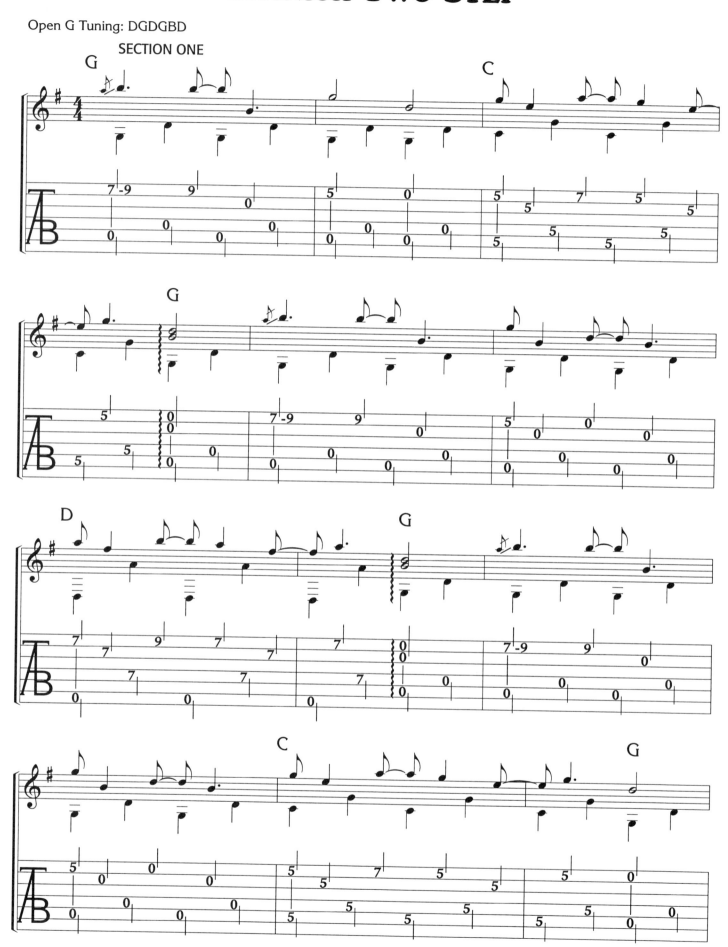

SECTION TWO

25

It Came Upon A Midnight Clear

Open G Tuning: DGDGBD

ST. LOUIS BLUES

Drop D Tuning: DADGBE

Stefan Grossman, Charlotte Doglio and John Fahey, Monte Porzio, Italy, 1982

photo by Jo Ayres

31

THE UNION PACIFIC

Open C Tuning: CGCGCE

Heavily   SECTION ONE

SECTION TWO

REQUIEM FOR JOHN HURT

Open C Tuning: CGCGCE

SECTION TWO A

F "IV Chord"

Only this note moves.

Many variations in performance

To Coda ⊕

TWO B ("First coming out")

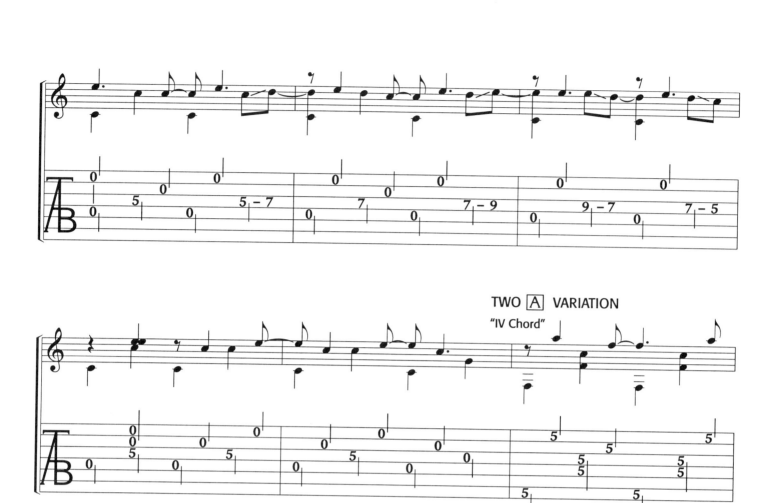

TWO [A] VARIATION

"IV Chord"

TWO C   (Occasional "Second coming out")

SECTION THREE

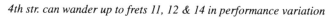

4th str. can wander up to frets 11, 12 & 14 in performance variation

SECTION FOUR

(variation)

42

AULD LANG SYNE

Open C Tuning: CGCGCE

John Fahey, Monte Porzio, Italy 1982

photo by Jo Ayres

STEAMBOAT GWINE 'ROUND THE BEND

Open G Tuning: DGDGBD

SECTION TWO

(Section Two is occasionally ommitted
going directly to Section Three (Middle)

(2nd time)

47

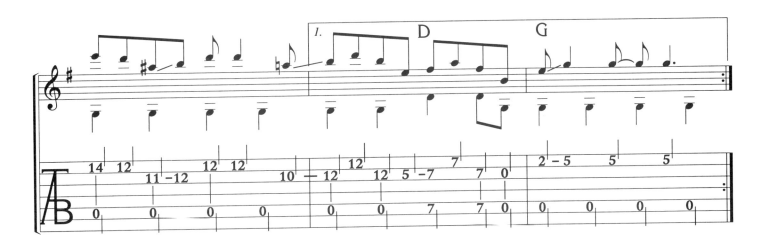

John Fahey, Rome, Italy, 1982

Silent Night, Holy Night

Open G Tuning: DGDGBD

OUTRO

Poor Boy A Long Way From Home

Open D Tuning: DADF♯AD

53